COUNTING CARS, TRAINS & AEROPLANES FOR KIDS

The perfect counting book
for children aged 2-5

Welcome to Vol. 1!

LEARNING THE KEY SKILLS OF SEARCHING, FINDING, OBSERVATION AND COLOUR RECALL!

Best of luck!

WE'RE GIVING AWAY OUR FIRST DIGGER STORY BOOK FOR FREE AT NCBUSA-PUBLICATIONS.COM

Are there **more road signs** or **more spaceships?**

There are

 **4**

and  **2**

signs **spaceships**

Which means that there are more **road** signs than **spaceships!**

How many green cars are there?

1   2   3   4

There are

4 green cars!

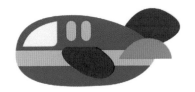  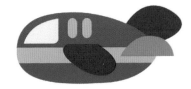

How many blue aeroplanes are there?

There are ② blue aeroplanes!

1   2

Count the
Rockets!

There is just one
Rocket

1

How many boats can you find?

There are 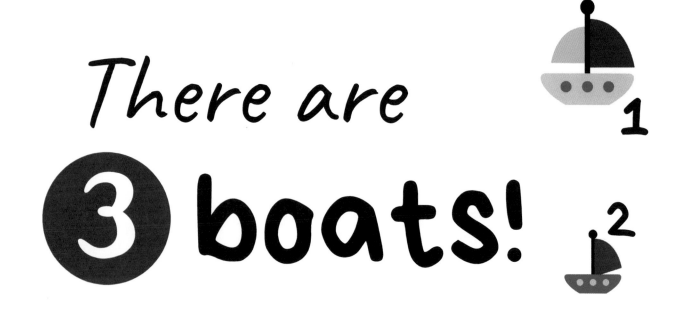 **3 boats!**

How many did you count?

How many trains can you count?

There are
4 trains!
Did you find them all?

1 **2** **3** **4**

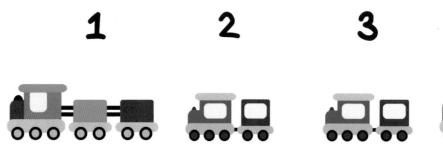

Count the red cars!

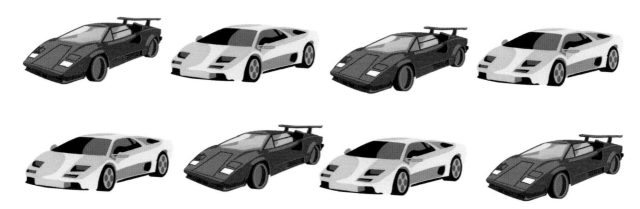

There are **ten red cars!**

10

1   2   3   4   5

6   7   8   9   10

That's a lot of cars!

How many
hot air balloons
can you find?

There is only

1

hot air balloon!

Can you see **more trucks** or **more helicopters?**

There are

8 and **7**

trucks   helicopters.

So there are more trucks

than helicopters!

Did you get it right? Get ready for the next counting question!

How many of the items fly in the sky?

 a rocket

flies in the sky

 a helicopter

flies in the sky

 a hot air balloon

floats in the sky

3 *So three of the items*
fly in the sky!

How many **cars?**

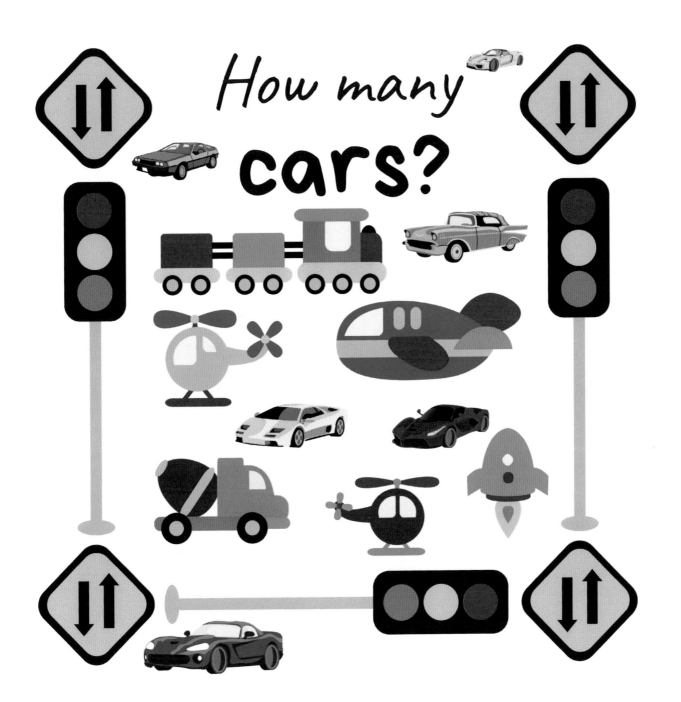

There are six

6 cars!

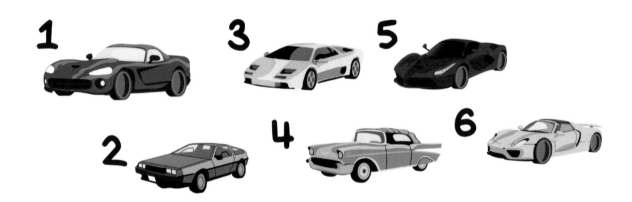

1

3

5

2

4

6

Did you find the small
yellow race car at the top?

How many can sail in the sea?

The **number** is **one!**

1

only the sailing boat...

How many of the items go on the road?

Five

5

Can drive on the road!

1 **2** **3** **4** **5**

Remember, the train goes on railway tracks!

Count the
traffic lights!

There are two traffic lights!

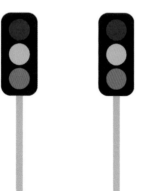

red - stop
yellow - wait
green - go!!

The last question!

Count the number of **road signs** in the whole book?

(including the one on this page, and including those on answer pages!)

How many did you count?

The answer is.....

14

Count The Diggers, Dumper Trucks & Tractors!

Printed in Great Britain
by Amazon